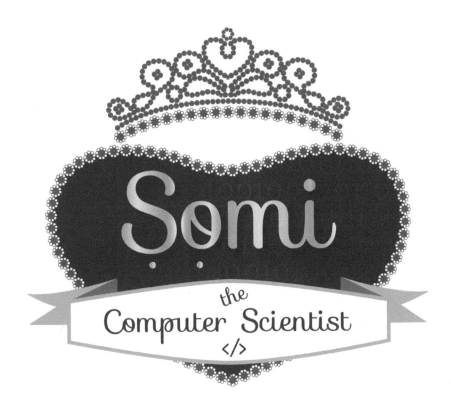

Princess Can Code

<Part_one/>

Written by Bukola Somide

COPYRIGHT

DEDICATION / ACKNOWLEDGMENT

I dedicate this dream fulfilled to my lovely and wise daughter, Olusomi. My very own princess Somi to whom I leave this legacy.

First and foremost, I thank God for the birth of this vision.

I acknowledge the support from loving friends and family. Your encouragement, valuable feedback, advice, prayers, and belief in my dreams is most appreciated. I especially recognize the following, "Destiny Helpers", who played a critical role in the fulfillment of this project. Adebolu A., who is wise beyond his years, helped his Aunty recognize the much-needed change in point-of-view of the narrative and scenes to elaborate on. Muyiwa Somide, who's gifted in graphic design anchored the book cover and back page designs, and layout. Esther Zufelt, an accomplished author who spent time driving many miles on multiple occasions to help edit the manuscript and held me accountable until it was complete. Finally to you, the reader, I hope you find this book educational and entertaining. Aspire to be excellent, believe in yourself, and create/code something innovative.

God bless you all.

"To become successful, seek to be a person of value.
Discover your unique gift.
Your gift makes you valuable."

§ Dr. Myles Munroe

This educational and entertaining storybook belongs to:

_____

I aspire to be a

_____

Meet Somi

Hello there! My name is Somi [shaw-me] Lovelin. My parents say I am a bright, young lady. I love dancing, singing, playing with my friends, and most especially solving problems through computer programming. My Mom loves her job as a Lead Software Engineer at Innovant Technologies. My Stepdad, who I call Dad, is a successful Music Producer. I also have a baby brother, Sola [shaw-la], whom I love so much. My parents are from Nigeria. They value education and respect, which plays a major role in the way I am raised.

Somi's Curiosity

It's summertime! Mom says it's our civic duty to help other people, so this summer I am volunteering to read storybooks to younger kids at a community center nearby. After story time one evening, Mom and I are walking back home. I am wearing my favorite pink sneakers with bow laces and a white T-shirt that reads, "Princess Can Code." I love the heart-shaped African-print knee patches Mom sewed on my pants. We get to a traffic stop. I can feel Mom's eyes staring at me but I am completely lost in deep thought, looking at the light up ahead.

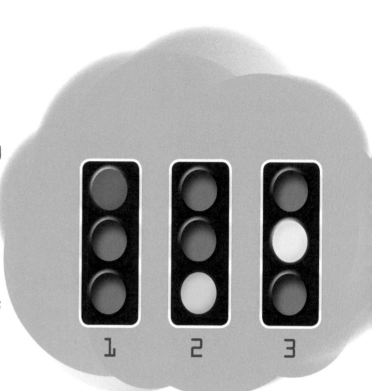

"Uh oh, Somi. You have that look on your face again, honey. What is it this time?" Mom asks curiously.

"The light up ahead...it's built with a program that loops*. The loop has three choices: green light, yellow light, and red light. Right, Mom?" I ask.

"Yes, dear," Mom replies. "Good job linking the computer programming concept of loops to a traffic light. I'm glad you have a natural curiosity to learn programming. Keep it up! I'll test your knowledge of these concepts later."

Just then, the traffic light turns green and we both start crossing the street. "I'll be ready," I whisper to myself while smiling from cheek-to-cheek.

Birthday Planning Mode, Activated

"Wakey, wakey! Do you know why today is so special?" Mom asks as she walks into my bedroom. I am used to Mom waking me up in the morning, but today is different. She's up SUPER early, on a Saturday.

"Oh my god," I grumble. I feel her warm body next to mine as she sits on the bed, and then she starts tickling me. I giggle uncontrollably, trying to catch my breath. "Stop, Mom," I cry. I secretly love when she wakes me up like this. It's fun. Click! The imagery light-bulb in my head lights up. "Yep, I'm awake now," I think to myself. I jump up from under the covers, doing my shimmy-dab dance while singing, "What day is it? It's my birthday. I'm gonna shake it like it's my birthday."

Mom laughs at me of course. "Yes it is, dear," she agrees. "Happy 8th birthday!" We quickly say our morning prayers and head off to prepare for the party. Oh yeah! Mom and daughter super birthday planning mode, activated.

Cookies, Pies, and Loops. Oh My!

Cookies, meat pies, fish rolls, and a layered banana cream chocolate chip chunk cake. Say that three times for a tongue twister. Mom and I are baking all sorts of goodies in the kitchen. "Mmmm, it smells so good in here," I think to myself. "I love cake. Weakness alert!" Suddenly, Mom interrupts my yummy fantasy.

"Somi, what is a loop?" She asks boldly. She does this on occasion to test my knowledge on computer programming concepts but this time, I am ready. Let's do this!

"A loop is a continuous cycle (iteration*) through a list of instructions or steps (procedures*)," I say with confidence.

"Good! I see you've been studying. Also, the program exits the loop if a statement (condition*) is false," Mom adds.

"Oh yea," I remember. "So if the statement, Mommy is beautiful, stays true then the loop goes on forever. Well until Mom gets mad at little innocent me then her beauty disappears, the loop stops, and the computer program crashes," I say as I laugh out loud.

"Ok!" Mom replies. "Look at you, Ms. Smarty Pants. Creative example," Mom laughs as well.

CODE ZONE

```html
<!DOCTYPE html>
<html>
<body>
<p id= "displayContent" ></p>
<p id= "displayContent2" ></p>

<script>
var somisBehavior = 'good', count = 1;
while ( somisBehavior == 'good' ) {
    //comment: Display content Mommy
    //is beautiful
    document.getElementById(
    'displayContent').innerHTML +=
    count + ' Mommy is beautiful.<br>';

    //comment: after 5 counts somi is naughty
    //so Mom becomes upset
    if(count == 5) {

        //Reset the value to naughty to exit the
        //while loop
        somisBehavior = 'naughty';
        document.getElementById(
        'displayContent2').innerHTML =
        'Mom is upset at Somi.';
    }
    //comment: increase count by one
    count = count + 1;
}
</script>
</body>
</html>
```

Score! Cool points for me. Whoop, whoop! I pat myself on the back.

"You've been so good this summer, dear. Helping with chores and reading to kids at the community center. So, guess what?" asks Mom. "Your Dad and I have a very special surprise for you today."

I am so excited I almost knock down the pan of warm cookies cooling on the counter top.

"Hey! Be careful now, Somi. Calm down, calm down. Ok, go get washed up and dressed, your party guests will be here soon," Mom cautions.

I say with a smile, "Thank you, Mom. I love you both so much." I give her the biggest kiss on the cheek and the warmest hug ever. You'd think I just passed a hard test, and in a way, I did and I was expecting to get what I had worked so hard for. I start rushing from the kitchen towards the bathroom yelling, "This will be my best birthday ever!"

Here Comes Princess Somi

   I am sitting at my silver desk in the bedroom, wearing a colorful Ankara-print princess dress. Mom *is* stretching my hair for the birthday party. It takes a while but it's worth it. I love my natural hair. It amazes me how my long coils can go from a little past my collar bone to my tailbone when stretched. Coily hair magic in full bloom! With half of my hair up in a big bun and the rest down my back, the final look is coming together. As I look into the mirror, I notice that Mom has tears in her eyes. It starts to concern me. I ask, "Why are you crying, Mom?" Hoping she's ok. She simply smiles and quickly wipes her tears with her right hand.

   "You look so wonderful, honey. You are all grown up," Mom says softly. "Oh, I have one more thing to make this look perfect".

   My eyes light up. I think to myself, "What could it be?"

   "Here it is," Mom says as she pulls out a beautiful tiara from a purple and gold velvet box. I was not expecting this.

   "Wow. It's the prettiest tiara I have ever seen," I say dreamingly. Mom carefully places the tiara on my head.

"Perfect!" She says. Mom looks so happy.

"Thanks, Mom," I reply. "Wait a minute, is this the special surprise you and Dad had for me?"

Red alert! I start feeling a little sad. I was expecting something way cooler, something I asked for during the school year. It is one of the reasons I worked so hard to earn it.

Mom, sensing my disappointment, quickly says to me. "Can't have Somi upset on her birthday. Cheer up, sweetheart. We will give you the special surprise after your guests leave. We want you to enjoy your friends without any distractions, ok?"

"Please, please Mom. Just a little peek. I won't tell," I beg. I'm hoping Mom will give in.

"Let me think about it.... Nope!" Mom says, smirking.

"Oookay, but why do I have to wait all day?" I complain.

"It's more fun this way," Mom replies while laughing but I am not happy. "Actually, your Dad and I want to spend quality time with you after the party. Just us, the Lovelins. Ok?"

That put a little smile on my face. I love playtime with my family. Dad is super funny.

"Ok, Mom. I'd like that," I answer. I get up, give her a hug, and off I go to party with my best friends. Let the Royal Ball begin.

Princess Somi's Royal Ball

I cannot contain my excitement. I hop, skip, and twirl from the bedroom to the living room and through the sliding glass doors into the backyard. All the princes are wearing suits and the princesses are wearing pretty dresses. A banner hangs over the patio which reads, Princess Somi's Royal Ball.

Under the canopy, there is a long dining table with seats for nine guests. The table is set with a white cloth, pink skirt, and draped with purple linen. The pastries that Mom and I made look so delicious as centerpieces. A couple of my friends are chatting by the cotton candy station. Some are having fun at the gaming machine and others are dancing on the dance floor.

I join my best friends, Esie and Noah, at the dining table. We share fun stories about school, our teachers, and families. It's time to cut that yummy layered banana cream chocolate chip chunk birthday cake. With my besties on both sides of me, we smile for the camera, cheesing from ear to ear. Picture perfect! A birthday fit for a princess.

"The ability to innovate stems from a creative imagination.
Nurture your intellect.
Read and be inspired."

§ Bukola Somide
(10/23/2017)

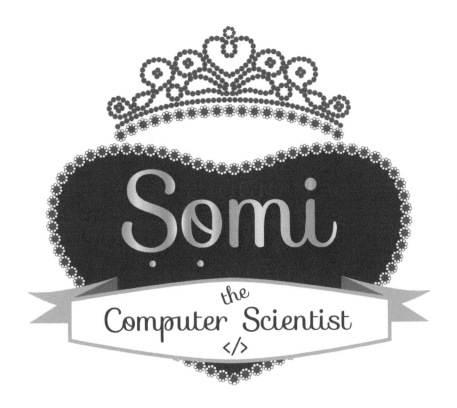

Princess Can Code

<Part_two/>

Written by Bukola Somide

The Birthday Surprise!

It is dark outside now. I cannot believe my birthday party is almost over. I wish it would never end. My friends rave about the Royal Ball to their parents and to each other. I am exhausted but very happy. I plop down on the living room couch to rest a little.

"Honey. Sweetheart. Somi!" Mom says loudly. She hovers over me trying to wake me up. I open my eyes, then I see my Dad holding a pretty pink and white polka-dot box with a cute bow on top.

"It's time, Princess," Dad says softly. "Open your surprise."

I am a bit sleepy but that won't stop me from finally uncovering this mystery. I quickly get up from the couch, grab the gift, and start tearing off the polka-dot gift wrap. Just then, I open the box.

"Yes, yes, yes. My very own Computer!" I scream, almost waking up my baby brother in the other room. I hold it above my head like I just conquered the world. It is a pink tablet with a sticker that reads, Nexon. Not sure what that means but who cares, I got what I asked for.

"I must admit, your Mom is the mastermind behind this gift. I just paid for it," Dad laughs as Mom pokes him in the arm. "I see a lot of great qualities of your mother in you, Princess. I'm proud of your hard work and persistence."

With tears streaming down my face, I give my parents a huge hug and say, "You are the best parents ever. Thank you, Mom and Dad. I wouldn't trade you, even for a slice of cake." We all burst out laughing together. Yep, I love cake a lot.

There's More.

"Let me show you one more surprise," says Mom.

"Really? There's more? What else could it be?" I wonder. Mom powers up the tablet. She lays it flat on the coffee table facing the ceiling.

"Watch this," she says as she clicks on an App. Suddenly, a three-dimensional projection floats above the tablet. It is a digital image (rendering*) of a female face.

"Hello, Somi," the image spoke, unexpectedly. I am in complete shock. My mouth is so wide open, it could touch the floor.

"I had the same look on my face when your Mom introduced me to Nexon. So, what do you think?" Dad asks.

"Nex...Nex...Nex what?" I stutter as Mom laughs at me with excitement.

"This is a Next Generation AI* IDE* Interactive Hologram, or Nexon for short. A pet project I've been working on for a few years now. Wear these smart gloves so you can interact with it." She grabs a white and purple color pair of gloves from the gift box.

"Wow, AMAZING!!" I react. It's hard to speak about Nexon without totally geeking out.

"I knew you'd love it," says Mom.

Yep! Score one-hundred points for my parents. Best. Surprise. Ever.

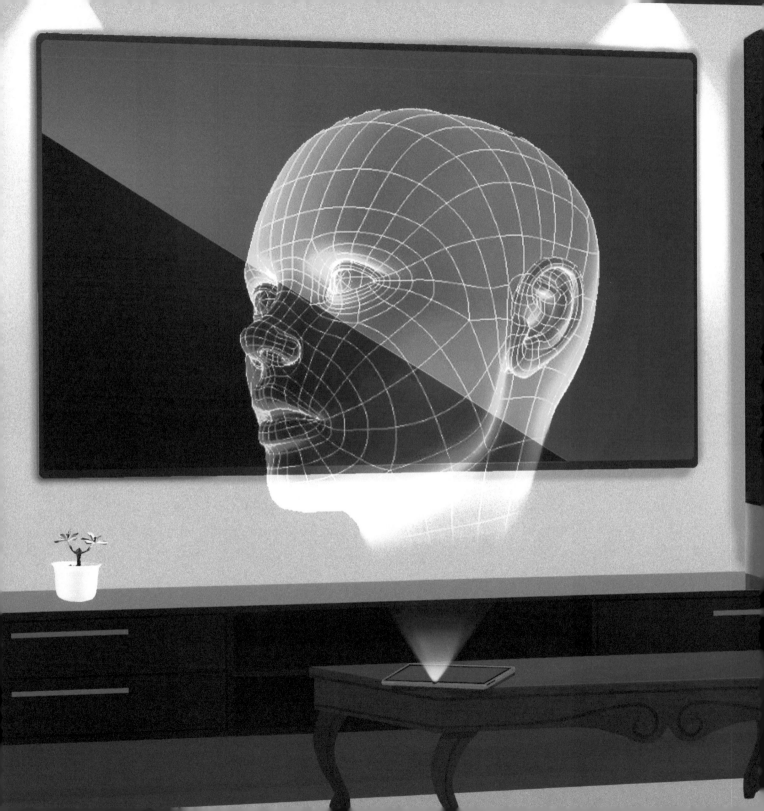

<code>Hello, World!</code>

Mom clicks a button, then Nexon asks with a computerized voice, "Would you like to write your first program?"

"Yes, yes, of course!" I say loudly.

"Indoor voice, honey, so Nexon can read your voice commands correctly," Mom cautions.

"Ok. Let's begin," Nexon replies. Then it opens a projection of a text-editing program. "Awaiting your command, Somi."

I am looking a bit lost at this point. I ask, "What do I say?"

Mom answers, "Relax, honey. There's a manual in the box with all the instructions and commands you can use but first, let's create a quick computer program. Remember the 'Hello, World' website we wrote a few weeks ago?"

I reply, "Yes, I do. We created a web page* that displayed whatever content we wanted." I put on the smart gloves with a little help from Mom.

"Yes, dear. Go ahead and type on the projected keyboard. The gloves have built-in sensors that recognize whatever holographic image you touch, then it sends commands to Nexon to process (compile*)," Mom instructs.

"Cool gloves," I think to myself as I stare at them, curiously.

Suddenly, it all comes back to me. I start typing code on the holographic screen. After a few minutes... "There! All done," I say proudly.

"Congratulations, Princess! You just wrote your first computer program with Nexon," Dad says while sitting on the couch watching us, his two favorite ladies in the world. "So what programming language is this?"

"HTML5*. Happy Text Markup Language," I say with a smirk.

"Um...not quite, dear. The 'H' is for Hyper not Happy," Mom says, slowly.

I reply with a silly voice, "Gotcha! I knew that." We all burst out laughing at the same time.

It's bedtime now. I cannot stop thinking about the party. I say my prayers, remembering to be thankful for my birthday, friends, and loving parents. Oh! Can't forget Nexon and the many computer programming adventures we'll create together. Best. Birthday. Ever.

CODE ZONE

```html
<!DOCTYPE html>
<html>
<head>
  <title> Somi's Game House
  </title>
</head>
<body>
  <!--Comment: navigation menu
  using hyperlinks-->
  <div>
    <a href= '/index.html'>Home</a> |
    <a href= '/images/birthday.html'>
    Birthday Pics</a> |
    <a href= '/coding-games.html'>
    Coding Games</a>
  </div>
  <h1>Hello, World!</h1>
  <p>Princess Somi Can Code.</p>
</body>
</html>
```

Web Browser

— ○ ×

Somi's Game House ✕

  (i) file:///C:/webpage/myFirtWebsite.html ◉ ⋮

URL

Home | Birthday Pics | Coding Games

Hello, World!

Princess Somi Can Code.

Web Page

Coding Exercise: Create your First Web Page

1. On your computer, open a simple text editor (eg. Notepad)

2. Copy code from code zone into a text editor

3. Save the file by clicking on the File > Save As menu option

4. In the dialog box, Enter this "myFirstWebpage.html" for the filename

5. Select "All Files" for the "Save as type" or extension type

6. Click "Save" button

7. Find your file on your computer, and double-click on the icon

8. Congratulations! You just created your very own web page.

Visit www.compsciabc.org and www.w3schools.com/html for more information and practice exercises.

Somi

the
Computer Scientist
</>

Programming
Adventures

*Şọmi's CompSci Knowledge Bytes

AI — stands for Artificial Intelligence. It often represents sophisticated (at times complex) programs that could collect data from the Internet and the user; capture it in a data storage, then applies built-in logic to correlate data to predict patterns, solve problems and more. Essentially, a software program that is built to process information like a human.

Binary Numbers[1] — Computers today use digits to represent information — that's why they're called digital systems. The simplest and most common way to represent digits is the binary number system, with just two digits (usually written as 0 and 1). Data in a computer is stored and transmitted as a series of zeroes and ones. For example, translate the number value 8 to its binary equivalent 01000.

* Starting from the right, express the base 2 version of the position from 0 to 4 (increase the number for higher values): 2^4 2^3 2^2 2^1 2^0
* Calculate the math for each position (e.g. $2^3 = 2 \times 2 \times 2 = 8$): 16 8 4 2 1
* Identify which digits added together would give you 8, represent that position with 1 for on or 0 for off: 0 1 0 0 0

Compile — The process of translating any computer language or command into machine language that a computer processor uses. The software program that performs this function is called a Compiler.

Condition — A conditional statement (if 2>1 then y ="hello") or expression that equates a hypothesis to true or false conclusion.

Educational Resources & References:
1.   "Binary numbers." Binary Numbers – CS Unplugged, https://www.csunplugged.org/en/topics/binary-numbers/ March 11th, 2018.

*Ṣọmi's CompSci Knowledge Bytes

GUI — Graphical User Interface, which is a visual display of functions a user can interact with to access features of a computer program. It employs graphic elements (e.g. dialog boxes, buttons, menus, icons, etc.) instead of plain text to allow users to trigger commands to the computer or to manipulate what is on the screen. For example, a login page could consist of text boxes to collect a username and password then a button that when clicked, submits a command to log into the program.

HTML[2] — Hyper Text Markup Language is the standard markup language for creating Web pages. It describes the structure of a Web page using elements/tags. When viewed in a web browser, the HTML tags are not displayed but instead the tags are used to render the content of the page.

Javascript [3] — is a programming language to program the behavior of web pages. It's inserted (injected) into HTML code

IDE — stands for Integrated Development Environment. It's a single software application that provides various tools needed to help to develop and test computer programs. An IDE normally consists of a source code text editor, a compiler to translate the code into a common computer language, a debugger to help find errors (also known as bugs) in the program and more. A developer accesses the IDE through a graphical user interface (GUI).

Iteration — the process of repeating a series of steps or procedures until a condition is satisfied.

Loop —A programming concept where a program continuously executes a sequence of instructions or procedures until a condition is false. There are different types of loops (while loop, for loop, for each loop, and do while loop).

Educational Resources & References:
2.   "HTML Introduction." Introduction to HTML, https://www.w3schools.com/html/html_intro.asp March 11th, 2018.
3.   "JavaScript Tutorial." https://www.w3schools.com/js/default.asp March 11th, 2018.

*Şọmi's CompSci Knowledge Bytes

Procedure – A group of programming statements or instructions that perform a specific task.

Render – A programming terminology used to describe the process in-which content/data is being written or drawn on the screen or user interface (UI).

Tags[2] – HTML tags label pieces of content such as "heading" (<h1/>), "paragraph" (<p/>), "hyperlink" (<a/>) and many more.

- <!DOCTYPE html> declaration defines the document to be a HTML5 markup language instead of the standard HTML

URL – Uniform Resource Locator, which is often referred to as a web address. It is a unique reference to a file located on the Internet (computer network). URLs are used to open websites, download images, videos, software programs and other types of files hosted on a server.

Var – a generic declaration of a data type. Variables are containers used to hold data values such as: x=2. 'x' is the container and '2' is the data value. This specific data type is known as an 'int' which represents small whole numbers. Other data types include 'string' for text values (string action="happy"), 'float' for number fractions/decimals (float y=3.14159) and so on.

Web Page – is a hypertext document commonly accessible through the Internet using a web browser (e.g. Internet Explorer, Google Chrome, Firefox, Safari). The web browser connects to a web page using the URL address.

Educational Resources & References:
2.   "HTML Introduction." Introduction to HTML, https://www.w3schools.com/html/html_intro.asp March 11th, 2018.

As a special thanks for purchasing this storybook,
you get to download a **FREE audiobook.**
Voiceover by the author herself, Bukola Somide

Go to this link to get your free audiobook while available:
www.bukolasomide.com/audiobook

Download Audiobook